The New Thought Christian

William Warch

Founding Minister
Church of Christian Living
Santa Ana, California

Other books:

I LOVE YOU

How To Use
YOUR TWELVE GIFTS FROM GOD

THE
NEW
THOUGHT
CHRISTIAN

William A. Warch

DeVorss & Company, Publishers

ISBN: 0-87516-591-5
Library of Congress Card Catalog No.: 77-90209

Sixth Printing, 1996

DeVorss & Company, Publisher
P.O. Box 550
Marina del Rey, CA 90294

Printed in The United States of America

To Connie, Chris, and Bonnie,
Three lights in my life.

Table of Contents

Introduction

There is a quiet revolution taking place throughout the world which is in reality a sign of spiritual growth. Many people are breaking away from traditional dogmatic religious beliefs declaring that, "It isn't right for me." Yet within the heart of these individuals is the conviction that there is a God or Supreme Power that they wish to relate to. These people seek a new definition of God, Christ, and Holy Spirit. They seek a loving presence rather than one that triggers guilt and duty. They dare to ask questions and challenge traditional values. Fortunately, some have discovered new ways on thinking new thoughts on God which make common sense.

You may be seeking more satisfying explanations and more meaning in your relationship to God. If you are open to new possibilities and new thoughts as to your spiritual development, you will probably gravitate toward a New Thought center or church.

This book is an explanation of what a New Thought Christian is. There are New Thought Christians in New Thought centers and churches throughout the world. These centers and churches may have names like Unity, Religious Science, Divine Science, or they may be one of the hundreds of independent New Thought locations.

The "International New Thought Alliance" is an international association of New Thought centers and churches, with headquarters in Scottsdale, Arizona. Worldwide activities are published in the I.N.T.A. magazine, THE NEW THOUGHT QUARTERLY. The great forward direction of the New Thought movement can be read in the pages of this QUARTERLY from the articles authored by the leaders in this field. An annual International New Thought Congress is sponsored by the I.N.T.A. at various locations throughout the country, attracting thousands of New Thought leaders and students. Mini-Congresses are held in various regions of the country throughout the year.

A complete collection of the past works of New Thought authors is held in the Unity Library in Missouri. Many inspirational publications abound from the various New Thought institutions. An inspirational daily message is provided to over three million readers in the monthly magazine, THE DAILY WORD, published by Unity School of Christianity, Unity Village, Missouri. Another popular publication by them is UNITY, A WAY OF LIFE. Religious Science International publishes, CREATIVE THOUGHT, an excellent small magazine of daily inspirational messages. The Divine Science Churches publishes a similar inspirational magazine, ASPIRE TO BETTER LIVING. The SCIENCE OF MIND MAGAZINE combines monthly articles along with daily messages and is offered through the United Church of Religious Science. Hundreds of books and other magazines can be found at local New Thought centers and churches.

This has all come about by people that feel that God is more than a judgmental overseer in the sky who sends some people to heaven and others to hell. There is a greater definition for man than "sinner". The New Thought Christian knows he is great and wonderful!

What Is God?

PREVIEW

1. God is neither person, place, nor thing.

2. God is man's potential.

3. God is invisible energy-intelligence.

4. New Thought is a scientific approach to God.

5. Consciousness is the degree of your God-awareness.

6. God is omniscience, omnipresence, and omnipotence.

The previous page of this chapter is the best possible description one can give of God. Any further explanation reduces and distorts the vastness and purity of God. The following pages will be filled with words and ideas and descriptions which are an honest attempt to describe the nature and character of God. But for the best possible description of God, return to Page 6. God is neither person, place nor thing. But mankind has always tried to identify God as such due to the way the human mind operates. The human brain is a fabulous device but is limited in its present stage of development. No matter what level of development you are in, this is where you must begin in your search for Truth and for your understanding of what God is.

God is absolute and therefore can bear no descriptions. It is erroneous to describe God as strong or loving or wise. God is actually Strength, Love, and Wisdom. God is every good attribute you can name and much more. Using adjectives to describe God is man's way of personalizing and identifying God in the attempt to comprehend God's nature. The author will, of course, revert to descriptions because that is the function and purpose of this chapter, to describe God.

God is invisible energy which permeates all that is. This energy is also intelligence and power. It is the absolute which underlies all creation. However, it does not create. It does not need to create, therefore it does not create. Mankind has needs so man creates things with his thoughts and feelings. But God does not. The great breakthrough for an individual is when he realizes that God is all potential. God is your potential and is the source of everything you need. If you need power you draw it from absolute power, God. If you need love, you draw it from absolute love, God. There it is, simply waiting as potential for you to draw upon.

Any concept of God that separates you from seeing God as your invisible source of good, separates you from your good. Some people have worshiped rocks. Some have worshiped idols while others have worshiped the weather. Some think of God as a large man-like figure in the sky, far removed from mankind. The idea that God is invisible intelligence, energy and love could shake a person to the core. It may be too illusive to comprehend and man is sometimes more comfortable with tangibles. It is for selfish convenience that people worship objects or other people. Usually the motive is for ego reassurance, not the desire to grow in the comprehension of the character and nature of God.

If you were to take a table and crush it to pulp and finally reduce it down to its molecular structure, you would see that atoms are at the base of its makeup. But to take it a step further, if you could smash the atom, releasing and converting it back to pure energy, it would be once more in that raw state of energy-intelligence. So it is with all things. Everything you know of in your manifest world is derived from God as energy-intelligence. God is man's potential just waiting to take shape and form according to what man thinks he needs. In this invisible state of all potential, there are twelve characteristics that best describe the nature of God. These are faith, strength, judgement, love, understanding, will, imagination, power, order, zeal, renunciation, and life. *

---

* For more in depth study on these twelve characteristics, read William A. Warch, How To Use YOUR TWELVE GIFTS FROM GOD. 1976. Christian Living Publishing Company. 140 South Beth Circle. Anaheim, CA 92806

The term "New Thought" comes from the courageous view that one should constantly be receptive to new thoughts of God. You do not understand God fully and certainly literal biblical descriptions do nothing but terrorize the soul. It is time to combine science with your personal intuition and willingly accept new mind expanding ideas about the true character of God. If you are willing to free yourself from the idea of a vengeful scorekeeper in the sky, you are a likely candidate to be a New Thought Christian. If you are willing to eliminate any idea from your mind that separates you from your invisible source, you are becoming a New Thought Christian. If you are willing to get rid of the idea that it is God's will that you should be poor and miserable, you are just on the verge of becoming a New Thought Christian. A New Thought Christian is truly willing to look at modern day science and see that religion and science are merging into the same study and will ultimately come up with the one answer that God is the cause of all things.

Since "God" is a word which is usually thought of as the name of a superior somebody in the sky, other alternatives should be considered. Such words as Father, Divine Mind, Being, Creator, Source, Jehovah, Elohim and Absolute Good have been used to name God. But to this author the word, "Spirit" best embraces that which is invisible energy-intelligence. You must come to terms with your own concept of God, but be sure you do not impose a limiting name on it or you will lock yourself into a fixed position. The New Thought Christian must be willing to grow in consciousness, and words and concepts have a great deal to do with your consciousness development.

The word "consciousness" refers to the degree to which you think and feel God. It does not refer to how much you know about God. Truth students know about God, but the New Thought Christian thinks and feels God, Spirit, through his entire being. The more you express (press out) God-like characteristics through your consciousness, the more highly developed your conscious becomes. /You are a point of awareness in the mind of God. You are part of the only species on earth that has self-awareness. You are the only type of animal on earth that is aware that it is really spiritual in nature. You are part of mankind which is the only species that has attempted and succeeded in lifting its level of awareness over a past level of consciousness. You are becoming aware of the fact that this is the greatest goal possible - - to grow in spiritual awareness. No wonder that during your spiritual pursuit you ask, "What is God?" Because the answer to that question unlocks the door to yourself, reality, fulfillment, and the kingdom of heaven.

God is omniscience, omnipresence, and omnipotence. Omniscience means all knowledge. All knowledge is the Truth that we all seek. Therefore, it is God that we seek in our quest for Truth. Omnipresence means everywhere present. This too is God. God is neither here nor there, but everywhere. There is no space in between molecular structure where God is not. So everywhere is not where God is, it is what God is. God is beyond time, space, or place. God is. God is omnipotence. Omnipotence means all power. There is no energy or inertia that is not of God. Even though these descriptions seem to divide God into categories they are all the same. Omniscience is omnipresence and omnipresence is omnipotence. It is all one. It is all God and God is all (Refer to Page 6).

How does the New Thought Christian comprehend this allness in developing conscious awareness of God? Through study, prayer, meditation and living experiences. All four will quicken an inner activity that will draw your focus of attention from outer things. Your questions as to what God is will launch you on an inner journey that will take you through every stage of development necessary to find the answer. The best manual possible to assist you on this journey is the Holy Bible, metaphysically interpreted.

If someone asks you, "Are you a Christian? Do you believe Jesus died for your sins? Are you born again and know that you are a sinner and live with a good deal of guilt and shame?", you can honestly answer, "Even though I may not believe in those humiliating details, I am a Christian. I am a New Thought Christian because I am developing an awareness of God and my true nature."

SCRIPTURES

"The Lord your God is God of gods, and Lord of lords." (De. 10:17)

"The people that do know their God shall be strong, and do exploits." (Da 11:32)

"Hold thy peace at the presence of the Lord God." (Zph. 1:7)

"The Spirit searcheth all things, yea, the deep things of God." (1 Co. 2:10)

"There is one body, and one Spirit." (Ep. 4:4)

QUESTIONS

1. Is God a superior being?

2. Is God strong and loving?

3. Does God create?

4. What is man's potential?

5. What does "New Thought" mean?

6. What is meant by "consciousness"?

7. What is omniscience?

8. What is omnipresence?

9. What is omnipotence?

10. Are you a Christian? Explain.

DENIAL   There is no void in my life.

AFFIRMATION   God is, I AM.

Where Is the Christ?

PREVIEW

1. The Christ is in mankind.

2. There are three phases to your being: spirit, soul, body.

3. All God-qualities are in you as the "word" of God.

4. A blessing is the sending of Christ energy and love.

5. The "only begotten son of God" is the Christ idea in you.

The arrow of Page 14 is pointing at You! It is the single most complete answer to the question of where the Christ is. You could point to a rock or a tree and claim that the Christ resides therein because it is made of the same energy-intelligence as a human, but you would be wrong. The Christ resides within every human being and only there. You see, the Christ is a point of awareness in the mind of God. That is exactly what you are in reality, a point of awareness in the mind of God. A tree or a rock is not aware of itself. A tree and a rock are fulfilling all that they are meant to be. They are expressing fully what God intends, so conscious awareness is unnecessary for them. But man is not fully expressing all that he really is. This point of awareness is the Christ within every human being. Some people may not be consciously aware of it, but they literally carry God within their consciousness. Everywhere you go, God is. Not only as invisible energy-intelligence, but as life itself. The Christ within is really your true essence and all the rest of you is a container with a personality. Vain people often fall in love with each others' personalities and physical bodies and miss the Christ essence entirely. The most unfortunate situation is when one falls in love with his own personality or body. He then rivals his true self, the Christ.

Many years ago a man named Jesus discovered that all his potential was actually within his own being. He could actually say that God was within him and that he was within God. He had the ability to set his own personality and body aside because He had developed full Christ awareness. He was advanced to the point where He knew that His thoughts and feelings directed the movement of matter and formed His world. A simple act such as walking on water was a minor thought choice but appeared as a miracle to those who were out of touch with their own

Christ light. Jesus made a direct connection in thought and feeling with God and devoted his life to teaching others how to do the same.

There are three phases to your being: spirit, soul, body. Spirit is that Godlike part of you which is the identical image and likeness of God. It is the real invisible you made up of faith, strength, judgement, love, power, imagination, understanding, will, order, zeal, renunciation, and life. The spirit phase of you is God in you and is commonly referred to as the Christ in you. A person, such as Jesus, who has developed the full Christ consciousness is one who has developed his awareness of these twelve God qualities. In reality, these qualities are perfect in everyone, but not everyone is fully aware of them. The first phase of you, your Christ self, is perfect and unchangeable. The New Thought Christian knows that the Christ resides within him. He also knows that the Christ is in every man. This is how he knows his oneness with other people, by beholding the Christ in them.

The second phase of you is your soul. It is you as a self-conscious being who is aware of himself as human and Spirit at the same time. Soul growth is synonymous with consciousness development because both relate to the degree to which one is aware of his perfect Christ self. Your individual awareness of existence includes your thinking and feeling natures at conscious and subconscious levels. Your subconscious level is mostly feeling and is where you hold your attitudes, fears, securities, and self evaluation. It is your goal in soul growth to convince your subconscious (your feeling nature) that you are the Christ: perfect, whole, and prosperous.

Where is the Christ? It is in you. It is God's perfect idea of himself in you. Just as all elements of the ocean are in one drop of ocean water, all that God is, is in you. God

16

can be referred to as Divine Mind. The word of God is an idea sent forth by Divine Mind and that word is the Christ in you. Just as every word you send forth contains your level of consciousness, the word of God, the Christ, contains perfection. This perfect word, or idea, is placed within all mankind. This perfect idea is the son of God, the offspring. Where is the Christ? Wherever you see a man, woman, or child.

Your consciousness and your Christ self are housed in a physical body. Wherever you decide to take your body is also where you take your self awareness. You are not limited by being in your physical body, however, due to the fact that as a spiritual being your awareness can be placed anywhere. Although you are located in your body in a certain city in a particular state, you can be with someone else in thought and bless that person. A blessing is the sending of Christ energy and love to someone or something. There is a natural tendency for the Christ in anyone to move out into expression. That is why a person gives you a loving response when you say that you love him. That response is his way of returning a blessing.

Not only are individuals growing in this Christ awareness, but all of mankind is growing. It is a collective awareness which is called race consciousness. Often the word gets out that there is a flu epidemic and mankind collectively accepts the idea. It is then in the race consciousness. At that point you as an individual have to be careful not to catch the idea of the flu or you will catch the flu. The New Thought Christian has caught the idea that he is the perfection of God and that perfection need not catch the flu. He has the power to image a shield about himself of light and love. No negative idea can penetrate that shield. Even though the race consciousness is filled with such ideas as death, illness, and poverty, every individual has the choice to draw upon the Christ power within.

There are times when you meet someone that you might think could not possibly have the Christ within him. Perhaps his actions reveal nothing but hatred and ugliness. This only shows one of two things. Either he has separated himself in thought from his Christ self or you are caught up in judging his personality by appearances. In either case, the Christ resides within that person and he is a perfect spiritual being. A person may be deformed or missing a limb, but he is whole and perfect in Spirit. It all depends upon his conscious awareness of his indwelling perfection.

Christ means the Universal Idea of Sonship and everyone is a member. The real you is your personal awareness of yourself as God. It is at this personal level that you experience God as deep emotion and thought. Even though God as energy-intelligence seems impersonal in concept, your personal contact with God is a warm loving experience. This is why so many people love Jesus. They actually see the Christ in him and experience God through him as well as themselves. The brighter your Christ light shines through your personality and body, the more loved you will be. People will see that the Christ resides in you. It is the goal of the New Thought Christian to help others realize that the Christ lives through them as well. Then they will see that the perfect idea of God in them is the only begotten son. The only begotten son of God lives in every human being in the world. The idea of God lives in every human being in the world. Everyone is heir to his Sonship whether he is aware of it or not.

The greatest goal a New Thought Christian can set is to develop awareness throughout the race consciousness. In developing your awareness of your Christ nature, you will discover that it lives inside you. This awareness is the most contagious idea in the universe. The greatest way to infect others is by being an example rather than a teacher. There are only a few that are really gifted teachers, but everyone is meant to be a wayshower by his example.

It takes courage and great awareness to say, "I AM the Christ". This is the "I AM" of you. This is the realization that there is no separation between you and God. Ask yourself when you are very still, "Who is God?" If you are very still, a voice from within will respond, "I AM". That response comes from deep within and this is your clue as to where the Christ is. It is the answer to that wonderful question and it is the answer to every need you will ever have. Here is a wonderful statement of faith. "God is, I AM."

Where is the Christ? Refer to Page 14. There is the answer. Better yet, looking in a mirror while asking that question will reveal the truth. Still yourself and stand before a mirror and then ask, "Where is the Christ?" This will help you actually locate the Christ. If you ask the question with your eyes closed, you will feel the answer just the same. But if you want to develop conviction and courage look into the mirror and declare, "I AM the Christ." Every cell in your body will respond to the truth of your being.

SCRIPTURES

"We dwell in him, and he in us, because he hath given us of his Spirit" (1 Jn. 4.13)

"Awake thou that sleepest, and arise from the dead, and Christ shall give thee light." (Ep 5:14)

"The Father dwelleth in me, He doeth the works." (Jn. 14:10)

"Now, O Father, glorify thou me with thine own self with the glory which I had with thee before the world was." (Jn. 17:5)

"That was the true light, which lighteth every man." (Jn. 1:19)

QUESTIONS

1. Where is Christ located?

2. Is Jesus your savior?

3. What are the qualities of spirit in you?

4. What is meant by soul growth?

5. Is your awareness limited to your body?

6. What is meant by race consciousness?

7. What is the relationship between race consciousness and your consciousness?

8. Is a troubled, deformed person lacking in spiritual qualities?

9. Is your experience with energy-intelligence impersonal?

10. Is everyone meant to be a teacher?

DENIAL   There is no power that can hold my good from me.

AFFIRMATION   All things are possible through the Christ in me.

Who Are You?

PREVIEW

1. You are a process of becoming.

2. The object of your existence is to express God in all
    you think, say, and do.

3. The doorway to the invisible realm is the Silence.

4. You find your individuality in your oneness.

5. Individuality is the I AM, or Christ, in you.

6. You are the light of the world.

You are God's most wonderful idea. This idea is a perfect reproduction of Spirit, God, and is implanted within, waiting to be realized and expressed by you. This idea is called the Christ which resides in your body consciousness. This is who you are, a spiritual being housed temporarily in a wonderful body. But even though you are the Christ, you might not be fully aware of the fact. As you develop in awareness as an infant, you go through many stages of who you think you are and you are greatly influenced by your surroundings and the opinions of others. Therefore, your idea of yourself might differ from God's idea of you. In order for you to express your true self, you must consciously agree with God's perfect idea of who you are. Your soul longs to express itself perfectly and will cause dissatisfaction until you agree with God as to who you are.

You are a process of becoming. There is nothing fixed or permanent about you other than the perfect Christ idea within. Your conscious awareness and your physical body are constantly changing and adjusting toward the perfect expression of your Christ nature, Spirit. When you can say, "I and the Father are one", and fully accept it, you will express all good with no negativity. You will be expressing that which you are - - the image and likeness of God.

The object of your existence is to express God in all you think, say and do. Existence itself is the third dimensional realm where things are tangible, visible and formed. Reality is the realm in which the underlying truth to all things lies. This is the realm of the invisible, Spirit. Divine energy-intelligence, your Christ self, and God are all one in this plane and have no specific form or matter. It is the realm of divine ideas, and you are a divine idea God has sent forth. The third dimensional world of ex-

istence is a school for soul growth. It is where experiences are provided for you so you can meet and grow
through them. As you insist on meeting your opportunities
and challenges according to spiritual principles, you
grow in the awareness of your Christ nature. Without
existence and these experiences, you would not have the
opportunity to make these spiritual choices. Without
choice-making, there is no consciousness development.
A New Thought Christian is continually making choices
which adhere to spiritual principles rather than judging
by appearances. Who are you? You are a spiritual being
who is not preoccupied with lack, limitation, or whether
or not you can be harmed. You, as a New Thought Christian, are aware of the fact that as you recognize your
spiritual nature you are transforming your thinking, your
feeling, and every cell in your body. You are in an ever
constant process of change, a change which is moving
you as a third dimensional being into the realm of the
invisible.

The "way" that Jesus referred to was the way he lived,
thought and felt. Through leading a completely spiritual
life while in a body, his total being was transformed
back into the invisible realm of energy-intelligence, Spirit.
He did not go away or die. He is here, right now in the
invisible, urging us ever onward. We do not know how
many souls have completed the same journey, but we do
know that we are all on the same path. Each path is different, but they all lead to the same source - God.

The doorway to the invisible realm is Silence. You,
as a human being, are constantly dealing with the world,
your school for growth. But everyone needs a recess.
Everyone needs to take a break to be restored and re-
energized spiritually. Where does one go for this refresh-

ment? The world is all about you. Existence has you completely surrounded. But there is one place where you have
direct contact with God and that is through your spiritual
self, the Christ. In order to focus your attention on God
in you, the Christ, you need to still yourself and release
all outer concerns. You must go apart for awhile to this
silent place within so you can release your thinking and
feeling from the grips of the outer world of existence.
This is called, "entering the silence". This turning within
is your way of going through the door to the realm of
invisible reality and there you may drink of the divine
inspirational ideas of Spirit itself. After a time, you return
to the outer world to apply the ideas and principles that
you have gathered into your consciousness. The New
Thought Christian makes regular visits to the "Silence"
and in so doing, reminds himself of who he really is.
He is reminded that he is a spiritual being, living in a
spiritual world, governed by spiritual laws.

You find your individuality in your oneness. Everyone
is interested in his own identity. When you feel comfortable with yourself and feel you know who you are, you
are not subject to the opinion of others. They can neither
build you up with flattery nor tear you down with criticism.
If you are unsure of your true identity, you are vulnerable
to any strong personality that comes your way. You will
constantly try to please that personality by demonstrating
your abilities or you will shrink away feeling threatened.
In either case, you are in a precarious position when you
are not sure of yourself as a spiritual being. One thinks
of an "individual" as one who thinks for himself and
acts independently of popular opinions. When you listen
for inner guidance and act accordingly in the face of
opposition and appearances, you are acting as an individual. You are "centered" so to speak, and have a sure feeling of what you are doing because you are in conscious

contact with Spirit, God. You are not too concerned with whether or not it pleases others because you are interested in what is right and good rather than what is pleasing and acceptable. You may not be described as having the most colorful personality, but you most certainly will be recognized as an individual. Of course, it is not the recognition you are seeking. Your motive as a New Thought Christian is to develop your Christ awareness through your choice making in the school of Life. A beautiful thing begins to happen when you move through life as an individual. You see the Christ quality in others more and more. You feel one with them because you are dealing less and less with personality. It is in this close oneness with others that you respect others as individuals.

Individuality is the ⌐I AM,⌐ or Christ, in you. When you say, "I AM", and connect it with an idea, the Christ power moves it into expression through your consciousness. The I AM power is your Christ power. If you connect the idea of health to your I AM by saying "I am healthy", you will demonstrate health in your life. If you say "I am rich", you will produce tremendous prosperity in your life. The same holds true in negative choices as well. If you choose to think and say "I am sick and tired", you will become sick and tired. The Christ power makes no choices; it produces exactly what you connect to it in thought and feeling. Of course, your greatest and boldest affirmation is, "I AM the Christ". It is the truth and the more you know it, the more you express it. This helps you to express God in all you think, say, and do.

When you know who you are, you accept responsibility. The New Thought Christian literally speeds up his physical transformation and consciousness development through the conscious awareness of his I AM, or Christ self. By entering the silence daily, you are reminded that you are far more than a personality that has physical and emotional needs. You are the Christ, one of God's beams of light who is brightening the world and mankind into greater awareness. You are made of the same energy intelligence that holds the planets in orbit and breathes life into infants. Through constant realization of your divinity, you are bypassing petty grievances and 'ears and choosing to promote and express God's qualities such as faith, strength, judgement, love, power, imagination, understanding, will, order, zeal, renunciation, and life.

Who are you? You are the light of the world. This light is producing an image on the screen of the third dimension according to the way you feel about yourself. If you have a bad idea of yourself, your Christ light is projecting a negative personality and/or an ill body. If you feel good about yourself, your Christ light is producing a good personality with strong characteristics of a solid individual. If you feel God about yourself, your Christ light is expressing perfection in all you think, say, and do.

SCRIPTURES

"God said, let us make man in our image." (Ge. 1:23)

"I shall be satisfied, when I awake, with thy likeness."
(Ps. 17:15)

"As we have borne the image of the earthly, we shall also bear the image of the heavenly." (1 Co. 15:49)

"We all...are changed into the same image from glory to glory, even as by the Spirit of the Lord." (2 Co. 3:18)

"Christ, who is the image of God." (2 Co. 4:4)

QUESTIONS

1. Who are you?

2. Is there anything about you that is perfect?

3. What is the object of your existence?

4. What is meant by "I AM the way"?

5. What is the "Silence"?

6. What is the difference between personality and individuality?

7. What is choice-making?

8. What is meant by connecting an idea with your I AM?

9. How does Christ-awareness speed up consciousness development?

10. Does your self-concept affect your way of expressing?

DENIAL   There is no personality, opinion, or condition that interferes with my choices.

AFFIRMATION   I AM a spiritual being, living in a spiritual world, governed by spiritual laws.

How To Use Thought

PREVIEW

1. There is a three-fold nature to your mind.

2. Your Christ Mind is the realm of pure knowing in you.

3. Whatever you hold in your subconscious takes place in your body, affairs, and environment.

4. Thought is the mental activity which builds consciousness.

5. You have three directions from which to draw your ideas.

There is a three-fold nature to your mind. There is your Christ Mind, your subconscious mind, and your conscious mind. Of course, they are all one, but any explanation of the true nature of man will encompass the trinity. Usually the trinity refers to Father, Son, Holy Spirit. In metaphysics, one might say mind, idea, expression (manifestation). You might think of it as God, the Christ in you, and you as you consciously know yourself. The trinity seems to be necessary as a three-stage breakdown for your comprehension. Even when you consider yourself as an individual, you think of three levels: Spirit, soul, body. Being in the image and likeness of God, you find the trinity running throughout your being, even in your thinking and feeling. You have the Christ Mind, your subconscious mind, and your conscious mind. In reality, you have one mind, but this trinity explains the three divisions in which the human being seems to function in the realm of thought.

First there is God which is Universal Mind or Divine Mind. This is the everywhere-present Spirit of Absolute Good which is the very energy-intelligence that sustains every atom that exists. This is the realm in which resides every idea that God created as possibility. There is nothing left for God to create, for it is already done, complete and perfect. God's creation is perfect, whole, and yet invisible. It is every possible idea waiting to be shaped and formed by the thought and feeling of man. Universal Mind in you is the Christ Mind. Your Christ Mind is the first phase of your mind. Your spiritual development is not a matter of developing your spirit. It is already fully developed. Your spiritual development comes from developing your awareness of the perfection that already is. Since God is in you as Christ Mind, you know everything there is to know. Every God idea is at your disposal, every answer to your every question.

Your Christ Mind is your realm of pure knowing. You respond to the ideals of God by turning to the Christ Mind and laying hold of the ideas that make up your divine inheritance. There would be no consciousness without the movement of ideas in mind. The way you use these divine ideas will be determined by your level of thinking and feeling, or consciousness, and by your needs of mind, body, and affairs. The Christ is the deepest innermost you and functions at very low frequencies. These low vibratory frequencies are the most creative but can be overlooked when your attention is on outer things. As divine ideas are fed to you, you must slow down and quiet yourself to comprehend and use them. You need to attune your conscious thinking with your Christ Mind.

From this realm of pure knowing come your dreams and revelations. They are fed to you first through your feeling nature as intuition and then translated by your thinking nature into pictures and logical ideas. There is a never-ending reservoir of inspiration constantly afforded you, if you but turn your attention in the direction of your Source.

Perhaps it would be easier to comprehend yourself if there were only two aspects to consider, the Christ Mind and your conscious mind. But there is a part of you that functions beyond the now. It holds to memory and projects a future. It is your subconscious mind. It stores memories, emotions, ideas, attitudes, and concepts. It also does something that mankind has been trying to figure out for years. It computes all the input that has been consciously recognized by you and combines it with information from former lives and gives you a read-out called self-evaluation. This self-evaluation, or esteem, determines your present ability to express that which is in your Christ Mind. Fortunately you can effect your subconscious so that you may improve your expression of the Christ in you. Consciousness building has a direct correlation to elevating your opinion of yourself. The reason this is so important is that the Christ can give to you only to the degree that your subconscious will accept. If you feel you are worth only so much, that is all that will be manifest in your life.

Whatever you hold in your subconscious takes place in your body, affairs, and environment. Conversely, that which you have drawn into your environment, you may understand to be an indication of what is going on in your subconscious. This is a very valuable piece of information. If stingy people keep showing up in your life, guess what! There is a stingy part of you. A good way to verify this is to see if you can get an emotional rise when you come into contact with a stingy person. If you do, it is the stingy part of you saluting the stingy part of him. The emotional flare-up is a subconscious coverup.

Your subconscious is very creative. It will continue to create situations and draw mental equivalents until you grow through them. When you develop your conscious awareness of good in the situation, your subconscious alters upward. Whenever you grow, the other person will grow or go away. The situation will improve or dissolve. It has no choice. A good goal for one to set in soul-growth is to see that only good is stored in the subconscious. Since the Christ Mind is all good, it can express fully through a subconscious that has stored all good. Then every good thought that you consciously think will produce instantaneous results. The only delay in answered prayer is due to the clutter in your storehouse.

Now we come to the department of your mind where

you have the right to exercise your power of choice. This is in your conscious mind. This is where you are completely responsible for the thoughts you hold and how you use them. This is where you can actually decide which emotions to connect with your thoughts. Thought is the mental activity which builds consciousness. When you move ideas through your mind they become thoughts. Thinking is a process by which you are able to handle abstract ideas so as to form mental pictures and patterns. Once it is solidified in your mind, this pattern becomes the blueprint from which an outer structure is formed. All three levels of mind cooperate in forming outer structures. The conscious mind selects the designs, the subconscious mind accepts the design and forms the blueprint and the Christ Mind provides the power to bring it into manifestation, according to the blueprint. You can see what an important place the conscious mind has in its role of choicemaker. It is only at the conscious level where you can choose to alter the blueprints, or the subconscious mind.

You have three directions from which to draw your ideas. First, you can draw upon the outer world of impressions, facts, and conditions. These are things that you must deal with every day of your life. They are important but not to be mistaken as the best source of ideas. Nothing original can come from this direction. The greatest decision you can make in this area is to be very selective to harmonize with the good ideas and refuse to give power to the negative and limiting ideas.

The second direction from which you will receive ideas is your subconscious mind. This storehouse is full of ideas and impressions and your greatest decisions will come with regard to how you handle yourself emotionally as these ideas come out. The positive ideas will be expressed for constructive purposes of contributing to mankind and the negative ideas will be expressed so they may be dissolved and released from your consciousness. It is a cleansing process. Sometimes people misunderstand the negative feelings as they are being released. Any time you release a nagative idea from your subconscious, you will experience it in your feeling nature. Bless it on its way out, but don't let it frighten you. If you release it, it will no longer be a part of your subconscious.

The third direction from which you will receive ideas is your Christ Mind. This is the realm of all that is original and good, but unlike the subconscious mind, it will not impose itself on you as an overwhelming influence.

This is the unique feature about the Christ Mind. Although it has everything to offer, it gives you complete freedom of choice. In the outer world, people will exert tremendous pressure to get you to accept their thoughts. In your subconscious mind, you will receive even greater pressure to think according to what has been formerly stored up. But the Christ Mind offers the subtlest urging of all. It expects you to recognize your source of perfect ideas.

How are you supposed to use thought? You should use only the best ideas to move about in your consciousness. From all three directions, you must decide which are best, most meaningful, and productive in building your Christ awareness. Do you use thoughts that build your esteem? Do you express thoughts that reveal God-qualities to others? Do your words and ideas remind other people of their divinity? How do you use thought? You have complete freedom of choice, and it is through this choicemaking of ideas and thoughts that you build your awareness of what it really means to be a New Thought Christian.

SCRIPTURES

"Try me, and know my thoughts." (Pa. 139:23)

"Through wisdom is an house builded; and by under-standing is it established." (Pr. 24:3)

"A fool uttereth all his mind." (Pr. 29:11)

"Let the wicked forsake his way, and the unrighteous man his thoughts." (Is. 55:7)

"I know the thoughts that I think toward you, saith the Lord, thoughts of peace, and not of evil." (Je. 29:11)

QUESTIONS

1. What is the Christ Mind in you?

2. What is your subconscious mind?

3. What is your conscious mind?

4. How does your self esteem relate to that which you receive?

5. What part of you determines exactly what will manifest?

6. Who is responsible for the thoughts you hold?

7. What are the three sources of ideas you can draw upon?

8. What provides the power for the creative process?

9. Does your Christ Mind choose good for you?

10. How are you using thought?

DENIAL   There is no room in my mind for negative destructive thoughts.

AFFIRMATION   My mind is filled with the light of God; divine ideas are flowing to me now.

What Is Prayer?

PREVIEW

1. A prayer may be limited but never harmful.

2. There is power in the word of man.

3. Prayer has purpose.

4. You must discover the power of praise and thanksgiving.

5. There are many ways to pray.

Prayer is your conscious communication with God. It can be your expression of appreciation or asking to have a need met. But in either case it is the acknowledgement of Spirit, God, as your source of all good. Prayer is very important because it takes your attention from the world of appearances and places it in the realm of invisible reality. This very process of placing your attention on God opens you to the flow of all God's good. Your willingness to pray places you in a receptive consciousness.

There is an interesting paradox in considering the activity of God in responding to prayer. Even though God resides in stillness and we attune ourselves by stilling ourselves, the action of God is quicker than instantaneous. It seems to us that God acts faster than the speed of light in responding to prayer, but in reality that which has become apparent was there all along. What appears to be the activity of God is really the awakening of your consciousness to your good that has just been waiting to appear. It is a real breakthrough when you come to realize that all your prayers should be for the purpose of changing your consciousness. Rather than praying for health the New Thought Christian prays for his conscious awareness of the perfect health that is already his. His new awareness of perfect health allows him to accept the perfect physical transformation that must follow. If you have been disappointed in your search for joy and harmony it is because you have looked outside yourself for happiness. Even though energy-intelligence is without and within all things, your awareness is within you and this is where you must go in thought to make conscious contact with your source. The idea of your source being in a job, a salary, or residing on some heavenly cloud has a tendency to minimize the effectiveness of your prayers.

Some people are afraid that they can pray the wrong way and cause harm to themselves and others. A prayer can be limited but never harmful. By limited prayer, we mean prayer that is not aiming high enough. You have a tendency to ask for and expect only what you feel you are worth. This self-worth opinion is in your sub-conscious. Actually you are worth and could receive anything your heart desires. As you uplift your consciousness, you will receive more and more. You are God's perfect child and have already inherited His entire kingdom.

Don't be afraid of being specific in prayer. Being specific is not outlining. While some are afraid of outlining for God, they resort to vague requests and receive vague answers. Being specific does not mean that you cannot be receptive to greater ideas. If you visualize a new home in a specific way, yet remain open to the one you draw to you, your prayer is answered. At that point, you evaluate and decide whether it is the home you want. Perhaps it will stimulate new ideas to incorporate into your imagery. You may have many houses brought into your experience before you actually purchase one. The final home may be nothing like the original vision you held to but the specific prayer work activated energy-intelligence because you had conviction. If you had been outlining, you would have refused to look at any house that wasn't exactly like that which you had envisioned. You would have put a lid on your prayer. Prayers should include, "This, Father, or better".

Some people are afraid to pray for others, fearing that they harm the one who is prayed for. Prayer is not voodoo or witchcraft. It is your sending forth energy-intelligence as healing love to quicken the consciousness of that dear soul. If you prayed for harm to someone, the energy would remain within your consciousness, causing that effect to take place within you. God's will is a plan of absolute good for man and all creation. It is not God's will that anyone suffer. Your prayer is an energy boost for whomever you pray. It can only be directed for good.

There is power in the word of man. Every word you speak, every idea you send forth has power. If you send forth negative words and ideas, they re-cycle through your consciousness, supporting it and sustaining it as a negative consciousness. Negativity holds you at your present level of consciousness. But if you send forth constructive love-filled words and ideas, you are quickened in your awareness of Spirit. These words contain the character and essence of Spirit itself and they quicken the spiritual qualities in others. The greatest blessing you can give to anyone is reminding him of his spiritual nature. Prayer is the word and thought of man directed for good. It is, at the same time, conscious acknowledgment that the good is accomplished through the power of God. This good is the transformation of someone's consciousness, his understanding and acceptance of who he really is. All consciousness building comes from choice making. One must choose to send forth the powerful transforming word of truth to break up and destroy old limiting ideas of self.

Prayer has purpose. Understanding the purpose of prayer helps one live a more effective, meaningful life. The purpose of prayer is to elevate your awareness of your Christ nature. All prayer should be directed to God for the change of your consciousness. People often see a need in their life and pray for that need to be met. This is in perfect order but, unfortunately, they don't always realize that they must have an inner change in order to reach their good. For instance: if you come to the realization that you need more income to make ends meet, you need to pray for the purpose of expanding your consciousness. Where one person might pray for more money to come, the New Thought Christian prays to develop a prosperity consciousness. A prosperity consciousness is much more important than money because it causes the flow of money and good into your life. Ask yourself whether you pray for problems to be solved or whether you pray for the change of your consciousness. One keeps your focus to the outer while the other focuses you on your willingness and your relationship with God.

You must discover the power of praise and thanksgiving. Mankind in the past has been motivated to pray by the recognition of deficiencies in his life. Praise and thanksgiving are the other side of the coin for they cause increase and acceptance of your good. First let's consider praise.

When you praise something, you consciously recognize it as good in itself. Anything that you praise appreciates or increases. If you praise a child, he will appreciate it. The good in him that you are acknowledging will be quickened in his awareness and his chest will swell and a smile will come to him. Everything appreciates under praise. The human being in the past has had a tendency to focus on negative qualities but we are entering an era of recognizing our good. The New Thought Christian praises his health and prosperity. He knows how this increases awareness of health and prosperity and how this, in turn, causes increased manifestation of health and prosperity. If you have an old car and feel limited in having your transportation needs met, it is very important to use the power of praise. Praise the car and appreciate everything about it as you pray for your new car. The resentment of the old car will leave which frees you to increase your awareness of all the limitless possibilities coming your way. The trade-in value of the old car will go up in your consciousness and your opportunity to step into a newer car will present itself. Plants thrive on praise; animals thrive on praise; and so do your loved ones. In prayer, praise yourself above all.

The power of thanksgiving is another way to change your consciousness. You give thanks when you know you have received something. If someone were to hand you a pencil, you would say "thank you" after you had received it. You give thanks when you know you have it. This is your acceptance of it in your consciousness and once you have accepted it in your consciousness, you know it is yours. Once you accept anything in consciousness, it must manifest in your life. The New Thought Christian prays knowing he has already received.

There are many ways to pray. It is easy to get caught up in semantics so you must classify in your mind what prayer and its purpose is for you. Some say that negative statements are a form of prayer because negative results are brought forth. The very fact that you are putting forth the power of the word, negative or not, makes it a prayer. Some say that meditation is a form of prayer. Meditation is being silent and receptive to God's word for you. Therefore, it is communication with God. For some people, a scientific step-by-step method of prayer is necessary. For others, falling to the knees and folding the hands is comfortable. Is it wrong to cry and beg God for answers? Not if you are so moved that you need to break through a reserved play-safe attitude. It might be just what you need.

Ultimately, you must find your own way of communicating with God. You must find your way of getting beyond intellectualism and emotionalism, personality and ego, to your silent communion with pure energy-intelligence.

There seems to be four stages that the New Thought Christian goes through in prayer. What sequence and to what degree is an individual matter. First, there is the relaxation of the body. A tense body brings attention to itself and blocks the flow of energy. Second, there is a stilling of the mind and emotions. This takes a letting go of concerns and anxieties. It is placing yourself in the care of God. Third, there is your acknowledgement of God as your source of all good. It is in this stage where the request, the question, or the praise is given. Finally, there is the stage where even the request is released as you enter complete silence, that state of complete receptivity. It is in this silent presence of God that your inner transformation takes place. Perhaps there are no revelations, sensations, or inspired ideas that register in your mind - but you are nevertheless transformed. This is where your prayer is answered...in the silence of your own being. What is prayer? Prayer is communion with God in which you are transformed upon request.

SCRIPTURES

"Lord, I have called daily upon Thee, I have stretched out my hands unto Thee." (Ps 88:9)

"Blessed is the man that heareth Me, watching daily at My gates, waiting at the posts of My door." (Pr. 8:34)

"Daniel...kneeled upon his knees three times a day, and prayed and gave thanks before his God, as he did aforetime." (Da 6:10)

"Men ought always to pray, and not to faint." (Lu. 18:1)

"Ask, and it shall be given you; seek and ye shall find; knock, and it shall be opened unto you." (Mat. 7:7)

QUESTIONS

1. What does your willingness to pray cause?

2. How fast does God act?

3. If God is all about, why do you need to turn within to pray?

4. Can you harm another with inaccurate prayer?

5. Is being specific in prayer the same as outlining for God?

6. Who is harmed by your negative thoughts?

7. What is the purpose of prayer?

8. What do praise and thanksgiving cause?

9. Do you know which is the best way for others to pray?

10. What is your way of praying?

DENIAL   There is no separation between God, good, and myself.

AFFIRMATION   I am in constant communion with God. I feel his presence now.

Where Do You Find Balance?

PREVIEW

1. Balance is a prerequisite for inner peace and harmony.

2. Emotionalism and intellectualism prevent growth.

3. Balance leads you to stillness.

4. Stillness is your doorway to Spirit.

5. You must direct the energy flow of your God-given gifts.

There are a million things going on in the world and each of us comes into contact with a different variety of personalities. Not one of us has exactly the same worldly experience so, in a sense, each of us lives in his own world. Your world is the world you perceive and you have learned to deal with it as best you can. As you have come to discover yourself to be a spiritual being you have come into the awareness that this world of yours is but a reflection of your own consciousness. Earth shaking events reflect inner changes. Strong personalities reflect strong characteristics within yourself. There is a wonderful realization that comes to you when you see this connection between your consciousness and the outer world. You are awakened to the fact that if you change your consciousness you change your world and affairs. If you see that your outer world and life are out of balance you can call on your inner Christ power to change your consciousness. Finding balance within changes circumstances and events without. Where do you find balance? The only place you can find balance is within your consciousness.

Balance is a prerequisite for inner peace and harmony. This is the "kingdom of heaven" that you are seeking. There are four areas of balance you need to establish. First, you need to sort and find balance in your thinking and feeling. Second, you need to find balance between information you receive from intuition and information you receive through your five senses. Third, you need to find balance in your appetites: indulgence versus starvation. And fourth, you need to develop your awareness of your twelve spiritual powers and bring them into balance to realize the Christ consciousness.

Extremes in any area cause instability. It is easy to lose balance when it comes to intellect and emotion. When you are functioning with intellectual awareness and emotional stability you are centered. You are in a balanced state of consciousness and ready to focus on God. When you are swayed to pure emotionalism, your judgement is clouded and inharmony follows. The same holds true if you are prone to intellectualism. You lose your feel for things. Emotionalism and intellectualism prevent growth because either state pulls you off center.

Balance leads you to stillness. If you find yourself full of stress, anxiety, and concern, it is time for you to admit that you are very busy inside, worrying and experiencing fear. This is the time to slow down the busy streets in your mind and settle the tremblings in your heart. It is time to still yourself and find balance within. Perhaps you are overreacting emotionally or jumping to conclusions in your mind. More often than not, you feel you don't have time to slow down. But if you don't, you pay a terrible price. Use your mind to settle your feeling nature. Send forth positive words instructing your consciousness to become silent and still. Go apart and take a few deep breaths and utter these words, "There is nothing to be afraid of or concerned with because God is is charge of my life now". Take another deep breath and as you exhale, relax on the inside. Settle your emotions with loving thoughts directed to all those involved, including yourself. This is how you use your thinking to balance your feelings.

On the other hand, if you are feeling wonderful and someone brings in bad news or negative thinking, use your feeling nature to thwart the negative input. Instantly relax toward joy and love and do not resist or resent any statement. Love-filled nonresistance will permit negative information to pass on without lodging in your consciousness. This balance and stillness leads you to the threshold of pure energy-intelligence, the awareness of Spirit itself.

49

Stillness is your doorway to Spirit. It is all well and good to talk about God and spiritual activity knowing that it is a continuous activity, but unless you are involved in this spiritual activity, you can live in illness and limitation. This is why stillness is so important to you. Stillness is that inner position which encourages your receptivity to the flow of energy-intelligence. It is through this door that you receive your portion of your daily bread. This is how the love of God is channeled through you, by opening the door of receptivity. It is in this stillness and silence that your inner transformation takes place, enabling you to form and direct your good. You enter the chamber and close the door to the outer and then swing open the door to all that Spirit, God, has to offer. Within your consciousness is that place where you can close off existence and open yourself to invisible reality, energy-intelligence. It is very difficult, if not impossible, to find this point in your awareness when you are not still and you are out of balance in thought and feeling. You can think about Spirit but you can't actually experience it. Of course it is possible to feel the loving presence of God while driving along in a car, but that is not the same as your consciousness-transforming silence.

You must direct the energy flow of your God-given gifts. To bless someone is the sending forth of spiritual loving energy. When you do this, you are actually directing the flow of energy-intelligence. By accepting love you are directing loving energy through your receptivity. You are constantly sending and receiving spiritual energy by what you think, say, and do. There are, however, certain areas in your consciousness where you are more developed than others. Perhaps you are very loving yet not very patient. This means you lack in your awareness of strength. Perhaps you have an active imagination, but lack discipline. You are low in your awareness of order. You have a tendency to lean heavily on your God-given qualities in which you are highly developed. In the areas where you sense weakness you will resort to emotionalism. To attain the Christ consciousness you must seek to develop your awareness of the rest of them. Your subconscious will constantly draw opportunities and challenges so that you may develop your spiritual gifts in which you feel weak. If you are impatient and intolerant you will continually be confronted with challenges asking you to grow in your awareness of strength. If you are willful and manipulating you will draw your opportunity to become willing. If you are angry and unforgiving you will draw love challenges constantly. Actually, everything that comes to you in life is asking you to find perfect balance. This perfect balance brings with it inner peace and the conscious realization of your divinity. So everything comes to you for your good.

As you come into understanding that your challenges and opportunities are asking you to draw upon energy-intelligence for balance, you turn to your source more and more often. More frequently you still yourself so that you may close the door to existence and draw upon the invisible reality which is always at your disposal. This is where you still yourself toward God as strength or love or order or divine will. It is at this point of awareness that you seek to find, ask to be answered, and knock to have your consciousness opened. It is here where you are informed which qualities you need to develop. From this silent, still point in consciousness you draw upon energy-intelligence from the invisible to be used and applied in your world of existence.

It is phenomenal to witness your own transformation after you have stilled yourself toward love. You become so kind and thoughtful. It seems miraculous to develop knowing after you still yourself toward divine understanding. It is exciting to still yourself toward divine judgement and then move into making decisions and choices that lead you to success and happiness. But this is the way you direct the flow of your God-given gifts. And after you draw upon Spirit, you spend it by giving love, exerting yourself, and making choices. Your directing the energy flow of Spirit is your exercising of your spiritual gifts. This is exactly how you find balance in Christ consciousness.

SCRIPTURES

"Let me be weighed in an even balance, that God may know mine integrity." (Job. 31:16)

"A false balance is abomination to the Lord; but a just weight is his delight." (Pr. 11.1)

"Lord, now lettest thou thy servant depart in peace." (Lu. 2:29)

"If it be possible, as much as lieth in you, love peaceably all men." (Ro. 12:18)

"The kingdom of God is not meat and drink; but righteousness, and peace." (Ro. 14:17)

QUESTIONS

1. Should we all perceive the world in the same way?

2. How do you change circumstances and events?

3. What are some symptoms of intellectualism?

4. What are some symptoms of emotionalism?

5. Is balance related to stillness? How?

6. What is the doorway to Spirit? Explain.

7. Stillness is the position between what two realms?

8. How do you direct the flow of energy?

9. What is meant by "balancing your spiritual gifts?"

10. Why do challenges and opportunities come to you?

DENIAL   There is no room in my life for chaos; nothing can overwhelm me.

AFFIRMATION   I am calm and serene; the peace of God is filling me now.

Who Believes In Evil?

PREVIEW

1. Evil does exist.

2. No one is evil.

3. Evil is supported by negative beliefs.

4. There is one primary cause of suffering.

5. Agree with thine adversary quickly.

The question "who believes in evil" can stir a multitude of deep emotional after-shocks when pursued earnestly. Is it the cultist, the Russian, the mentally ill, or the entire human race? Is it YOU? Do you believe in evil? Do you believe it is a force on this planet which is seeking to harm innocent people who haven't the strength to save themselves? Probably the most pertinent question is whether or not you, yourself, actually believe in evil. Many say that there is no such thing as evil, that there is only good and God. Then others charge that the starving people and grotesque wars prove that evil exists. It is vital that you as an individual come to an understanding of what evil means to you and whether or not you believe in evil.

Evil does exist. This statement brings us back to the need to clarify the difference between reality and existence. In reality there is only good. This is the invisible realm of energy-intelligence from which all "things" come into existence. In this divine kingdom of light there is no evil, no negative, no error. This is God's perfect creation which is complete. From this perfection man draws forth his good into manifestation where things exist. Man who does not yet have complete awareness produces negative, evil results as well as good, harmonious results. Therefore, there is only good in reality and there is good and evil in existence. Evil is not real and must be artificially supported by negative beliefs. Good is permanent and evil is passing. Therefore, if you see something evil coming your way, simply allow it to pass by. It can't harm you unless you support it with your own negativity. Still yourself and say, "This too shall pass."

No one is evil. People often judge others as evil because they don't understand motives. You might even judge yourself to be evil because you do things that you don't approve of. You might claim that you do not believe in evil, but if you experience guilt, you believe in a form of evil. Anyone who believes that he is bad is supporting a belief in evil. Guilt is self punishment for being bad. This might look like an over-simplified statement but it is nonetheless true. Check yourself out. There are many mistakes you have made in life, most of which you have acknowledged and then moved right along. But those acts or mistakes that you made which were accompanied by guilt, were supported by the belief that you were bad for taking the action. Sometimes you make mistakes without guilt and sometimes you make mistakes with guilt.

The belief that you make mistakes will never harm you. The belief that you are bad, a form of evil, distorts your vision and self esteem. This belief will enable you to produce negative results in your world. Therefore, it is vital that you remind yourself of your true nature. The real you is the Christ, that same invisible energy-intelligence which is God. You are made up of the same stuff that God is, and that is nothing but Good. You are Good. You are not evil; no one is evil. You name people evil when you can't understand their negative behavior. Lack of understanding is not a good basis for good judgement. You call yourself bad when you do not understand your negative behavior. You have no right to judge others or yourself. You must forgive everyone of negative behavior and behold the Christ in them, especially yourself.

Evil is supported by negative beliefs. A belief is that which is held true. Once you accept something as the truth in your consciousness, it is a belief. A belief is an inner opinion and may be in your subconscious without your knowing it. All negative beliefs are erroneous, but they will prove themselves by producing negative "things" in the world of existence. The belief that you are bad is an erroneous belief, for you are in reality all good. But the belief itself can modify your behavior to where you do bad negative things. When you overcome your belief in evil and self condemnation, you will accept yourself worthy of all good. Then three things happen....your behavior changes, your self esteem goes up, and good things happen to you.

If all evil and its harm to you is supported by negative beliefs, then the way to eliminate evil from your world is to eliminate negative beliefs from your consciousness. This is done through a process of denial and affirmation (next chapter), prayer, meditation, and change of behavior.

There is one primary cause of your suffering and that is that you have lost sight of your divinity. Whenever you feel assured that you are a spiritual being and cooperate with spiritual principles, you experience no suffering. It results in a sense of well being, a feeling of good within. If things go wrong on the outer, this inner sense of well being carries you through until perfect outworking takes place. If you have forgotten that you are the living expression of God, there is nothing to carry you through negative appearances. You accept things at face value and must find some label for that which you don't understand. The label "evil" is put upon a person who does negative things that you cannot understand. "He does it because he is evil." We need an explanation for everything and "evil" and "bad" are explanations based upon ignorance. This is ignorance of what the true motives are and ignorance of the divinity in mankind. The primary cause of suffering is the separation, in thought, from God. Mankind has separated himself from or forgotten the Christ within. This results in a bad feeling which leads to the conclusion by many that they are, in fact, bad.

From the book of Matthew we read, "Agree with thine adversary quickly, whilst thou art in the way with him." Agreeing with thine adversary is insisting upon seeing that there is good behind all things. If a person is disagreeing with you, try to see his point of view. You may disagree with his opinion, but know that this person has the Christ in him and is good. If you find yourself in discord with his personality, you are likely to oppose him, thereby giving him the power to harm you. The same holds true of a condition. If you are experiencing financial challenges and find that you are opposing and fearful of them you give them power to harm you. The instant that you acknowledge that the condition came about for a good reason, one which will help you grow, the condition loses power and disintegrates. In either case you insisted upon seeing good at the base rather than evil. Agreeing with thine adversary is agreeing that it is only appearing as adversity and that underneath lies the opportunity to develop consciousness.

This brings us to the principle of non-resistance. Resistance transfroms your consciousness into a cobweb of negativity entrapping negative thoughts and feelings. If you physically relax in the face of adversity and still your emotions, there is nothing for adversity to feed on. When you still yourself you remind yourself of your divinity. From that point of view you see the truth behind appearances. Resistance comes from the belief in evil and that you can be harmed. By dissolving that belief you avoid useless pain and suffering. Non-resistance is a mental and emotional attitude of spiritual balance. Non-resistance does not mean that you never take action. Quite the contrary, you take action based upon a truth principle rather than emotionalism or intellectualism.

The word of truth always dissolves negative appearances and results in your personal growth.

It is your responsibility to prepare your consciousness for the acceptance of your outer good by seeking the ideas lying behind it. To experience prosperity you must accept God as your inexhaustible source of supply. To experience health you must develop a consciousness of health and wholeness. The belief in evil or the feeling of being "bad" interferes with your preparatory work. It blocks consciousness development. Ask yourself, "Do I believe in evil? Do I live with a sense of guilt over being bad because of mistakes I have made?" If you have this inner interference, remind yourself of who you really are and ask for self-forgiveness and guidance. It will come quickly because you are growing in your understanding of what it means to be a New Thought Christian.

SCRIPTURES

"Wickedness shall be broken as a tree." (Jb. 24:20)

"Yea, though I walk through the valley of the shadow of death, I will fear no evil" (Ps. 23:4)

"I say unto you, that ye resist not evil." (Mat. 5:39)

"If thine eye be evil, thy whole body shall be full of darkness." (Mat. 6:23)

"Be not overcome of evil, but overcome evil with good." (Ro. 12:21)

QUESTIONS

1. Is there such a thing as evil?

2. Is evil real?

3. What is the difference between reality and existence?

4. Why do some people call others evil?

5. What is guilt based on?

6. If you do cruel, evil things, are you evil?

7. What supports evil?

8. Does changing your behavior effect your self esteem?

9. What is the primary cause of suffering?

10. What is non-resistance?

DENIAL   No harm can come to me because I do not believe in evil.

AFFIRMATION   I am wonderful, fantastic, beautiful, and good. I am the Christ.

How To Form
Denials and Affirmations

PREVIEW

1. Denials and affirmations are tools for changing your consciousness.

2. Denials erase, cleanse, and release all beliefs, thoughts and concepts that are contrary to reality.

3. Affirmations are statements of truth by which you build a conscious awareness of God and an existence of all good.

4. Denials and affirmations seem to wear out.

5. Basic instructions on developing denials and affirmations for you.

Denials and affirmations are tools for changing your consciousness. Everyone wants inner peace and a sense of well being. This state of consciousness comes only when you are in the process of developing spiritually. Spiritual development comes with the choices you make in life and denials and affirmations are powerful choice-making tools.

When you become aware of the fact that you are not happy with life, the people around you, or conditions in general, you try to make changes. At first there is a tendency to change outer things but that doesn't seem to solve the problem. In fact, it is discouraging to realize that you are drawing the same problems time and time again. At times, it seems that all of existence is against you and no matter what you do there is just another problem to block your happiness. The New Thought Christian works on his own consciousness rather than trying to manipulate outer things because he knows all things are drawn to him according to his consciousness. So the more aware he becomes of the Christ, his real self, the more good and harmony will be drawn to him. So two things are accomplished when one develops spiritually. First, you grow in Christ awareness and second, existence changes and adjusts into harmony, abundance, and health. Denials and affirmations are two consciousness building tools that are used to alter your consciousness, not existence. The change in existence is a result of your inner change.

Denials erase, cleanse, and release all beliefs, thoughts, and concepts that are contrary to reality. You may ask how you can tell what needs to be eliminated from your consciousness. The answer comes from an honest appraisal of your inner feelings and outer conditions. Make a list of the things that disturb you, including your negative feelings. For every negative appearance in your life there is a negative equivalent inside. The important thing to remember in using denials is not to deny away the appearances but deny the inner belief or concept that supports that appearance. For instance, if there exists for you a condition where you don't have enough money, work on your belief in poverty and limitation rather than denying that you have a money problem.Instead of denying that you have a wart on your hand you deny permission for it to remain. Instead of denying that you feel lonely you deny the need to be alone. Denials are designed to erase negative inner conditions such as anger, hate, or fear. Forgiveness itself is a denial. When you forgive someone you deny the anger the right to reside in your consciousness. When you give love for hate or love for fear, you are forgiving them from your consciousness. Of course, you go through the process of forgiving some person but you are, in fact, forgiving yourself.

A negative consciousness is mental enslavement to anxieties, fears, frustrations, and limiting beliefs. This can be overcome when you are willing to accept the fact that it is your own limited pattern of thinking and feeling that is binding you and not people or things or circumstances. Denial clears the mind for the re-establishment of truth which comes by affirmations of good thoughts and feelings toward God, yourself, and your fellowman.

Affirmations are statements of truth by which you build a conscious awareness of God which results in an existence of good. They are very positive and orderly statements made silently or audibly so that the ideas may take hold in your feeling nature. They are the "yes" attitudes of mind that result in the acceptance of your good. This actually brings ideas out of God-mind into the realm of manifestation or formed things, existence. Not only is your awareness altered, so is your existing world. Affirmations cause change in you as you accept them as your own. These inner changes cause the rearrangement of inharmonious conditions to harmony and prosperity. Actually, you could say it is almost like brainwashing when you consider the cleansing activity of denials and the retraining of habits of thinking through affirmations. The only difference in this kind of brainwashing and that of wartime is that this transformation of consciousness is by the conscious voluntary choice to use the power of the word of God. Rather than a destructive process, it is a building process which takes place under the power of energy-intelligence.

Sometimes denials and affirmations seem to wear out. This is because they have served their purpose or you need a little more self investigation as to your fear. Never feel discouraged if your favorite denial and affirmation seem to lose their effectiveness. It is not a sign that you are losing faith or that affirmations don't work. It is more a matter of your old affirmation not suiting your new consciousness. Remember, every day you are growing and changing. With this change comes new understanding of God, deeper insight into yourself, and new challenges that you are now ready to face. Your old self may resist change and one of the ways to avoid change is to lose interest in making new affirmations. Your personal will has been responsible for self-preservation for a long time and it is reluctant to hand the reins over to your Christ nature. Discipline yourself daily to choose your new direction of growth. If you don't, other people will gladly inform you on how to grow according to their opinions.

Here are some basic instructions on how to form denials and affirmations for your personal use. First, detect what is bothering you or appearing in your life as a challenge. Everyone has some challenge or else he is not growing. Second, recognize the fact that there is some belief in you supporting this challenge so you, as a New Thought Christian, work on eliminating the belief in you rather than denying the challenge. Third, form your denial. This is the tricky part. Some people mistakenly try to deny away the old appearance. That is trying to manipulate the outer and only drains your energy. If you are afraid of a particular person and think he may physically injure you, you must deny that he can injure the real you. Of course he can break your arm and you know this. You would not believe your own denial if you said he couldn't. But you know that in reality he cannot harm the real you. Your perfect Christ self is unalterable so you can honestly say with all your heart, "He cannot harm me." You will be amazed by the fact that when you believe it, it becomes so. Silently repeating your denial builds a knowingness in you that will thwart your fear. Once your fear is gone, you refuse him the power to injure you physically as well as spiritually. The key is to use your denial on your belief, not on the outer appearance. If you have a wart, don't stare at it and say, "I do not have a wart." Of course you have a wart. But the real you has no imperfection and you can deny the need for any imperfection to blemish you. When you believe that nothing can blemish the real you, you will witness your healing. In seeking your perfect denial, you have the privilege of honestly identifying and releasing a negative quality or concept that you have been hanging on to. Speaking the words, silently or audibly, moves energy-intelligence into action to change consciousness and existence.

Wherever you create a vacuum by denial, you must fill the void with truth. This is your fourth step. This is what an affirmation is. It is a declaration of truth which replaces the old mistaken concept. Without the affirmation the old self will try to draw the old negative belief back in. It is the survival instinct once more. In developing your affirmation be sure that it is not designed to move outer things about. Use words that clearly denote spiritual principles so that you develop consciousness. Once you do this you can believe what you are saying. If you can't believe your affirmation, it won't be effective for you. For instance, if you affirm that you will have ten million dollars by noon tomorrow you probably won't get it. If you don't believe it yourself, it is a joke, not an affirmation. But if you claim that you are developing your ability to accept vast riches, you will see results very quickly. One is aimed at the outer and the other is designed to change your consciousness. You have control over the outer through your consciousness development and no other way. Here are some examples of denials and affirmations.

DENIALS

WRONG   I deny that I am broke.

RIGHT   Limiting ideas and feelings of frustration are now being dissolved into harmlessness.

AFFIRMATIONS

WRONG   I am going to have a handful of money when I open my eyes.

RIGHT   God's abundance is flowing to me now as ideas, love, and supply. I know it, I feel it, I see it in my hand.

After you have developed strong positive denials and affirmations, enter the silence awhile. Just as you would give yourself over to a doctor for physical surgery, you must give yourself over to God so you can be greatly affected without the busyness of your mind and emotions. If you ever feel you can't come up with denials and affirmations, just start writing. You will quickly see how they need to be reworked until you have developed just the right ones for you. The New Thought Christian knows that it takes discipline and preparation to develop consciousness. Remember, God's greatest gift to you is inspiration and your greatest gift to God is preparation.

SCRIPTURES

"And he said to them all, 'If any man will come after me, let him deny himself.' " (Lu. 9:23)

"All the promises of God in him are yea, and in him Amen." (2 Co. 1:20)

"These things I will that thou affirm constantly." (Ti. 3:8)

"Commit thy way unto the Lord: trust also in him; and he shall bring it to pass." (Ps. 37:5)

"According to your faith be it unto you." (Mat. 9:29)

QUESTIONS

1. What is the purpose of a denial?

2. How do you determine what you need to deny from your consciousness?

3. Should you deny that problems exist?

4. How does one forgive?

5. What is the purpose of an affirmation?

6. Can you alter outer things without changing consciousness?

7. What is meant by claiming your good?

8. Is it easy to change your consciousness?

9. What are the four steps in forming denials and affirmations?

10. Give a denial and affirmation that are beneficial in helping you to meet a current challenge. Did forming them help you in consciousness development?

DENIAL   There is no emotion, fear, or threat that can lock me into my present level of consciousness.

AFFIRMATION   Today I am transformed, uplifted and inspired by the mighty force of God working through me.

What Is Metaphysics?

PREVIEW

1. Man's attempt to understand his inner voice has created metaphysics.

2. There are three main branches of metaphysics: epistemology, ontology, and cosmology.

3. There are several doctrines of metaphysics.

4. Metaphysics and Bible interpretation go hand in hand.

5. The New Thought Christian is a metaphysician.

Man's attempt to understand his inner voice has created metaphysics. Many people go through life just taking
for granted those questions of existence, purpose, and
meaning that the metaphysician finds most puzzling.
Yet there are many more people that feel there is much
more to existence than survival and security. No matter
what social status or ethnic background, certain individuals have started questioning and searching beyond
the world of appearances and existence itself. There is
an inner voice, the intuition, constantly reminding you that
"There's more, don't accept this limitation, the physical
is not the beginning nor the end, there is that which is
beyond the physical. There is the metaphysical. Accept
nothing at face value because the potential is better than
the appearance. Keep going; you can make it. There is
nothing that can hold you down if you will accept the
invisible reality of all that you are." William James de-
fined metaphysics as "nothing but an unusually obstinate
effort to think clearly".

"The Metaphysical Poets" is the name given to a group
of English poets of the 1600's, the most influential of
which was John Donne. He wrote both religious and non-
religious topics. Metaphysical poetry explored the phi-
losophical problems of the one and the many, unity and
division, and the spirit and the flesh. The metaphysical
poets often ignored traditional stanza forms. They used
vividly colloquial language, irregular rhythms, clever but
obscure or outlandish imagery, and extravagant diction.
Critic Samuel Johnson first used the term "metaphysical"
in describing the group and criticized them for what he
felt was an excessive use of learning. In the 1900's the
essays of T. S. Elliot helped stimulate interest in meta-

physical poets. His writings helped set the stage for the New Thought movement which was struggling to find itself among dissatisfied orthodox Christians.

There are three branches of metaphysics: epistemology, ontology, and cosmology. Epistemology is the study of knowledge, ontology is the study of the nature of things, and cosmology is the study of the arrangement of the world and universe. It is not vital that these "ology" branches are commited to memory, but it is important that the New Thought Christian is not deceived into thinking that metaphysics is limited to religion. To the contrary, metaphysics is an approach to religion borrowed from philosphy. Daring to look beyond literal fundamental Christian beliefs makes the New Thought Christian a metaphysician. He is an explorer of self and universe rather than a dogmatic believer.

To complicate things more, there are many doctrines of metaphysics. Briefly these are Idealism, Absolute Idealism, Supernaturalism, Naturalism, and many more. The main thing to keep in mind is that the New Thought Christian obviously falls into the category of metaphysician because he is dealing in the realm that is beyond (meta) appearances (physical) and is interested in the order of the universe. He understands that there is one source and that his conscious contact with this invisible source lies within himself. He also seeks to understand underlying principles so that he may cooperate with them in order to uplift his consciousness.

Charles Fillmore, co-founder of Unity School of Christianity, defines metaphysics in this manner. "The systematic study of the science of Being; that which transcends the physical. By pure metaphysics is meant a clear understanding of the realm of ideas and their legitimate expression." He describes a metaphysician as "one skilled in the science of Being; a student and teacher of the laws of Spirit." Ernest Holmes, founder of Religious Science, uses a scientific approach to analyze Spirit metaphysically. This is shown in his Chapter 1 heading of his text, THE SCIENCE OF MIND: "The Thing Itself, The Way It Works, What It Does, and How To Use It".

Metaphysics and Bible interpretation go hand in hand. The true nature of man and his creator is always revealed through anything which man builds, writes, and does. Any thorough analysis of man's writings will show what he is thinking and believes. A study of his cities reveals much the same thing. Close scrutiny of his behavior will reveal his innermost thoughts and needs. It is only natural that the inspired writings of the Bible hold within them the secrets as to the true nature of Man, his source, and the principles under which he functions. All of man's creative endeavors hold within them man himself. Even fairy tales reveal the fears and dreams of man and child. It is beneficial, therefore, to look beyond the literal meanings of the Bible to the metaphysical meanings of the characters and the events therein. Within the preface of Unity's METAPHYSICAL BIBLE DICTIONARY, we find this paragraph:

"Apart from its being a book of great historical and biographical interest, the Bible is, from Genesis to Revelation, in its inner or spiritual meaning, a record of the experiences and the development of the human soul and of the whole being of man; also it is a treatise of man's relation to God, the Creator and Father ....."

The most astounding thing about metaphysics is that it is such a personal experience for each individual as he pursues the exploration of the nature of his own being. Each person finds his own unique truth as he understands what the Bible and its characters mean to him. Each discovery is a lesson that applies to something that is going on in the student's life that day. You can hardly turn to a page without finding that a particular passage will instruct you on how to resolve or dissolve a challenge in your life. It seems like magic at first. Then you come to understand that it is divine guidance that places your finger on a particular verse. It is divine wisdom that gives you the very meaning you need to understand. The most reliable source of inspiration you can find is within you. The second greatest source of inspiration you will come upon is the Holy Bible, especially when you move to a metaphysical (beyond literal) interpretation.

Who is the greatest authority as to its true metaphysical meaning? You are! Many forerunners such as Emmet Fox have interpreted beautifully and may help you to a point of departure, but the Christ in you will reveal the true meanings as you are led through the inspired writings of the Bible.

The New Thought Christian is a metaphysician. YOU are a metaphysician by every definition and classification if you are seeking to understand the nature of your spiritual self and you plan to adhere to spiritual principles in consciousness development. New Thought is not really so new, for men have been on this endeavor for years. But it is new in that it breaks away from the fundamental approach to Christianity: that Jesus is the only divine being to inhabit the planet earth. P.P. Quimby, the father of New Thought, considered Jesus to be a highly developed individual and the "Christ" as a science of self-discovery. About 1862 Quimby had a tremendous influence upon Mr. and Mrs. Dresser, Warren Felt Evans, and Mary Baker Eddy. These in turn influenced others until institutions such as Religious Science, Unity, and Divine Science emerged. A great number of independent churches have also been inspired to teach from the great wealth of metaphysical materials.

Probably the most incredible thing that a New Thought Christian discovers as a true metaphysician is that each individual is responsible for affecting the universe and mankind in the most positive way possible. It is part of God's divine plan that each of us discover himself as a very important channel of energy-intelligence. Here is a (new) thought-provoking poem which encourages you to join in God's divine plan for all mankind:

> "Who am I?" poor Moses cried
> That you have chosen me
> Can't you see how old I am
> and busy as can be?
> I'm not eloquent or wise,
> or know the promised land
> Choose another leader, God,
> I'm simply not your man."

> When Gideon was called upon
> to lead his tribe to war
> Said he, "I'm just a farmer boy,
> I've not done this before.
> I'm the smallest of my brethern,
> the least of all my clan
> Find another leader, God
> I'm simply not your man."

> How oft it is with us today
> when there's a need to fill
> We find a thousand reasons why
> we cannot fit the bill.
> But once we give ourselves to God

and enter in His plan
It isn't long before we know
we really are "His man".

Nita Buckley

SCRIPTURES

"When I consider thy heavens, the work of thy fingers, the moon and the stars, which thou has ordained; what is man, that thou art mindful of him?" (Ps. 8:3,4)

"In whose hand is the soul of every living thing, and the breath of all mankind." (Jb. 12:10)

"Be not conformed to this world." (Ro. 12:27)

"The things which are not seen are eternal." (2 Co. 4:18)

QUESTIONS

1. What has caused you to look beyond the appearances?

2. Did metaphysical poets start a religious movement?

3. What are the three branches of metaphysics?

4. Why is a New Thought Christian a metaphysician?

5. Name some New Thought leaders and their contributions.

6. What value is there in a metaphysical approach to the Bible?
7. Who has the final word on metaphysical interpretation?

8. Is New Thought new?

9. Who is the father of New Thought?

10. What responsibility do you have in affecting the universe?

DENIAL   I am not limited to appearances; there is no beginning or end to me.

AFFIRMATION   A divine plan is working through me now.

Where Is Jesus Now?

PREVIEW

1. Jesus is alive and well and living everywhere.

2. The Christ is perfection and is living in you.

3. There is no such thing as time or space.

4. All religions are trying to say the same thing.

5. God's divine plan is working through you now.

Jesus is alive and well and living everywhere. Jesus knew the truth and became the truth and lives in the midst of us as Spirit of Living Truth. It is a challenge to accept that an abstract idea can become a manifest thing or that a manifest thing can become an abstract idea. But things are moving from reality into existence and from existence into reality constantly. This is the process of transformation that is continually going on as you develop your consciousness. For instance, you have brought the idea of food, shelter, and clothing from invisible reality into your living experience, existence, by using your various spiritual gifts such as faith, imagination, and strength. Therefore, you have drawn your good from God to and through you. Every time you exercise your spiritual gifts you develop your awareness of your Christ self. As you develop spiritually, you are undergoing mental, physical, emotional, and spiritual transformation which is taking you closer and closer to living in reality rather than existence.

As you use the Truth you become the Truth. As you develop your awareness of prosperity, you realize that you are prosperity itself. Then, of course, you manifest prosperity in the outer. At the same time all concerns about prosperity diminish. As you develop your awareness of health, you realize you are perfect life itself. Then you manifest nothing but health in your body. So two things are going on at once during your spiritual development. First, good things are being formed from energy-intelligence while second, you are being transformed back into pure energy-intelligence at the same time. At first thought, this might be a little startling, but this is all you are in the first place. You are in reality a spiritual being, whereas your body and world of existence is your school for consciousness development. When you are fully developed, you will no longer need experiences, nor the world, nor a body as you know it. They will become useless and unnecessary to your perfectly developed consciousness.

Jesus developed to the point where he was transformed into pure living Truth which gave him conscious omnipresence, omnipotence, and omniscience. You too are pure living Truth but might not be completely aware of it. When you no longer express error, unkindness, or limitation, you will have complete dominion over reality and existence. Jesus is alive and well living everywhere but not in physical existence as far as we know. If Jesus were to manifest himself in existence, it would probably pull the attention of countless thousands of people to an outer personality. This is the last thing we need so we are urged by Jesus, and any others who might have reached conscious perfection, toward inner spiritual awareness. Anyone who is of high consciousness is a helper and an encourager to those about him. It only stands to reason that those who have reached perfection take on the purpose of urging all of mankind toward spiritual awareness.

The Christ is perfection and living in you. The word "Christ" is used in many ways. Some think of it as Jesus' last name or that Jesus had an exclusive association with the word. The New Thought Christian associates the word Christ with that perfect God part of you. God in you is your Christ self. It is who you really are, which means that you and your Father are one. God is your source and all that you are. You are in turn a channel through which God expresses all his wonderful qualities. When you turn within in thought, you contact the direct source of all that you are. If you still yourself to this Christ part of you, you become receptive to the wonderful urging and guidance that is constantly being supplied to you. Your obedience to this guidance causes you to bring your good to you as you are being transformed more and more from existence to reality. This entire process is the claiming of your divinity, your natural inheritance.

There is no such thing as time or space. There is only the here and now. In the world of appearances man has tried to make sense out of what he sees and experiences. So when he witnesses changes, he thinks in terms of the way it was and the way it is. In other words, man thinks in terms of when and where, then and there, which helps him make sense out of changing appearances. Anything that pulls you off the here and now puts you into the past or future in your thinking and this moves you into limited thinking. The only time you can do anything about your consciousness is right now. In fact, this instant is the very moment that you may alter your consciousness. You didn't miss your chance yesterday and you are not going to have another chance tomorrow. Yesterday and tomorrow are man's invention to explain the changes that are happening in consciousness right now. There is no other place other than right here. The material arrangement of houses and mountains makes it seem otherwise but in reality there is no place other than that place in God-Mind which you occupy. All that is, is consciousness, whether you are talking about reality or existence. All that is, is here and now, not when you get a lucky break. You have in your being every good thing or idea that you can imagine. Your good is ready and waiting for you to realize that you have it now, this instant.

Unfortunately, many people get locked into the idea that Jesus did the things he did then, long ago; therefore you get locked into the idea that the place that all the miracles took place was in some far off land. Miracles are taking place in consciousness here and now, not only in

Jerusalem 2,000 years ago. The belief in time and space lends beautifully to a myth of some personality having a second coming, when in reality the second coming is taking place in you here and now as greater awareness of energy-intelligence.

All religions are trying to say the same thing, but human beings have a tendency to recognize differences rather than similarities. There is a fearful need to be "right" rather than aware. You as a New Thought Christian may have a different definition of "salvation", "sin", "evil", "Christ", "God", and "suffer" than a fundamentalist. This does not make one right and the other wrong. It is just that you both have a different definition on your road to awareness. He has to make sense out of existence in the most meaningful way for him just as you are making sense out of existence in the most meaningful way for you. You are both motivated by Spirit whether you call it energy-intelligence or Jesus.

Full awareness of all mankind is God's divine plan and God's divine plan is working through you now. There are three stages in the betterment of mankind. First is that stage when you arrange material things to meet your outer needs. Second is that stage when you try to develop your awareness of your Christ-self because material things don't satisfy. Third is when it becomes your sole purpose to serve God and mankind because you have become selfless, fearless, and loving. Every choice you make in being patient, loving or giving is a contribution to the entire race consciousness. Personal growth is a contribution to universal growth. If you ever wonder how you can contribute as Jesus contributes, seek guidance from within. You will discover that the more light and truth you can express into the atmosphere the more everyone is uplifted. You will also receive specific instructions as to how, where, and when you may serve. Your intellect will interpret your guidance into these terms so that you can function at your present level of consciousness.

Where is Jesus now? He is residing in the consiousness of every willing soul as a great encourager, instructor, and wayshower. Just as your mother, father, favorite hero, or lover may reside in your consiousness, so may Jesus. His particular message is that the Christ is in you. He is cooperating with you in bringing God's divine plan into fruition.

SCRIPTURES

"My presence shall go with thee, and I will give thee rest." (Ex. 33:14)

"Fear not, for they that be with us are more than they that be with them." (2 Kings 6:16)

"For thy name's sake lead me, and guide me." (Ps. 31:3)

QUESTION

1. Can an idea become a material thing?

2. Can you, who live in existence, be transformed into the realm of divine idea?

3. What happens to you as you use Truth?

4. Where and when did Jesus go?

5. Should Jesus return to the physical dimension?

6. Is it necessary for you to be transformed from existtence to reality?

7. Why has man invented time and space? Can they be used for escape?

8. Can Catholics, Baptists, Jehovah's Witnesses, Jews and Metaphysicians all be right?

9. What is God's divine plan and how does Jesus fit in?

10. Does God's divine plan happen to you or through you? Give some specifics.

DENIAL   Nothing can come between me and my good, God.

AFFIRMATION   Light is filling me to overflowing.

Who Believes In Reincarnation?

PREVIEW

1. There is no such thing as death.

2. You experience many lifetimes without leaving this plane of existence.

3. Grace is the upliftment from bondage through greater awareness.

4. What is the purpose of your body?

5. Are you a "born again" Christian?

Do you believe in reincarnation? Do you believe that there is another living experience in store for you after you lay your present body aside? Or do you think it is all over when you "die"? If you believe that you have experienced a former lifetime, whether you remember it or not, you believe in reincarnation. If you believe there is another experience which will take you further in consciousness development, you believe in reincarnation. Reincarnation is the rebirth of the soul in a new body. Transmigration is the rebirth of the soul in a new body which may include lower animal forms. This chapter is not referring to transmigration when discussing reincarnation. Mankind and mankind alone is the channel of God's expression of himself as Christ. Lower animal forms are manifest outpicturings of man's mind as are trees, money, airplanes. You are co-creator with God of all manifestation and creation. Your pet turtle does not create the environment with his consciousness; in fact, he can be exterminated into extinction as a species if man so chooses.

There is no such thing as death. Man's greatest fear is of pain and of the unknown. Pain and the unknown have been mistakenly labeled "bad" because they arouse fear in mankind. Of course, we are coming into the understanding that pain is good as a warning signal that something is out of order. With no pain you could not detect malfunctions of your physical body or your emotions. Continued pain is suffering and it is illogical to remain in a circumstance of continued pain. In Truth, however, there is a good purpose to pain. Fortunately mankind is slowly coming to the realization that there is no such thing as death and this moves us away from one of the biggest pain producing misunderstandings. The belief in death automatically brings with it the fear of the unknown. It raises such questions as, "Where do I go when I die?"

"What happens to my soul if I were bad?" "Is there such a thing as hell?" "Does the real me go into extinction?" These are all unanswerable questions that are associated with the painful belief in death.

Your life is the life of God expressing through you. To imagine that life itself can die is irrational. This irrationality has existed due to the fear associated with not understanding the discarding of the body. You have endless lifetimes, many of which take place during this particular incarnation. There is a big transition in your soul growth when your body is put to rest but you have had many significant transitions during incarnations. They are significantly marked by the people you associated with during that period. These people were drawn to you due to what was going on inside you. If you were to write down the most significant eras of your life, you would have to admit that you were in many ways different from one era to the next. There is an odd feeling of loss or shock from one era to the next if you think back carefully. For instance: high school years, a marriage, a job change. These may represent eras that reflect levels that you have come through in your consciousness development.

To say that it is useless to lay the body aside would be foolish. We all know the importance of the "sabbath" or silent still times during the day. Obviously, when the body is laid aside there is a period of stillness where great soul assessment takes place until the next birth. That point between lifetimes is much like a wonderful meditation where there is a realization and renewal. Whether these assessments take place in a body or not is immaterial. It is all taking place in your consciousness no matter where you are.

There is strong evidence that the belief in the need to lay the body aside is losing ground. The longevity of

the human being is increasing; diseases are being con-
quered; and the consciousness of mankind is constantly
being uplifted at an accelerating rate. As the human body
is uplifted through consciousness building and regenera-
tion, the need to reincarnate is coming to an end.

Obviously each living experience is but a part of the
continuum of spiritual growth, with each lifetime being
the next opportunity to make new choices. One can never
tell at which level another person might be by appearances.
Every soul has its secrets. Perhaps someone is developing
an awareness of prosperity yet you would judge him to be
in poverty. The impoverished conditions were created
for his good and he might be of a very high consciousness
with this particular area to work out.

One subject that often arises with reincarnation is the
belief that you pay for the sins of your present lifetime
in the next lifetime. Also the burdens and sufferings of
this lifetime are payment for past sins. This point of view
is focused on negative behavior rather than degrees of
awareness. Grace is the upliftment from bondage through
greater awareness. If you have made a mistake, you do not
have to pay for it. Through Grace (greater awareness)
you are free of the limited thinking that caused you to make
the mistake in the first place. Knowing that God is a loving
force and not vengeful frees you to turn within for answers
that will uplift you. There is no payment necessary under
the law of Grace. Under the law of Grace you understand
the law of action and reaction, that every action has its
natural consequence. Spiritual insight frees you to take
the right action; therefore, "by the Grace of God" (of which
Jesus taught) the past does not determine what you must
experience in the present.

Everything is an embodiment of an idea. Your physical
body is the embodiment of your soul at its present level

of consciousness. You may ask what is the purpose of your body. It is the vehicle through which you relate to your world of experience. As the perfect container of your soul, it reflects that which it contains. As you develop in your spiritual awareness, your body is transformed closer to pure radiant energy-intelligence. Therefore, it is vital that you consciously care for your body. An unkept body will reflect the state of your soul. A clean orderly body is the reflection of an orderly consciousness. In the literal sense, cleanliness is next to Godliness.

So often the question is asked, "Are you a born again Christian?" In the way it is asked, this question usually refers to accepting Jesus Christ as your savior so that you are quickened by the Spirit of the Holy Ghost. But to the New Thought Christian there is an entirely different meaning to being born again. With each new awakening you are born into a new level of consciousness. In other words, you are constantly being born again as you develop in your awareness of the Christ within. This has nothing to do with Jesus other than the fact that he too entered a constant state of renewal. As you let go of old concepts and beliefs, you release who you were in the past and accept a new understanding of yourself. New ideas about yourself and God are constantly being born in you as your Christ nature reveals itself to you.

SCRIPTURES

"If thou wilt enter into life, keep the commandments."
(Mat. 19:17)

"Which were born, not of blood, nor of the will of the flesh,
nor of the will of man, but of God." (Jn. 1:13)

"Except a man be born again, he cannot see the kingdom
of God." (Jn. 3:3)

"That which is born of the flesh is flesh; and that which
is born of the Spirit is Spirit." (Jn. 3:6)

"Being born again, not of corruptible seed, but of incorrup-
tible." (1 Peter 1:23)

QUESTIONS

1. Do you believe in reincarnation? Elaborate.

2. Is the conscious awareness of God being developed
by dogs and cats as well as human beings?

3. Are pain and the laying aside of the body bad?

4. Can you die?

5. Do you have to be born into a new body every time you enter a new level of consciousness?

6. What happens between incarnations and what is the purpose?

7. Can you judge someone elses level of consciousness?

8. What is the law of grace?

9. Why do you need a body?

10. Are you being born again?

DENIAL   There is no need to suffer and there is no such thing as death.

AFFIRMATION   There is one life, that life is God's life, that life is my life now.

How To Become Prosperous

PREVIEW

1. There are overwhelming similarities **between** God and money.

2. Prosperity and fear have their roots in your subconscious.

3. Give to the point of complete commitment.

4. Never save money.

5. There are three levels of giving.

Prosperity is a sense of well being. No matter what the outer conditions may be, if you have an inner sense of well being, you are prosperous. You may wonder how one may maintain this prosperous feeling if the outer looks like there isn't enough supply to meet one's needs. It comes in the realization that God is the source of all your good. This realization alters the outer conditions to where food, clothing, shelter, and money come into your living experience. The reason that it is so easy to become confused as to your true source is that there are likenesses between God and money.

There are overwhelming similarities between God and money. Money is a symbol but seems real while God is real and often seems like a symbol. In reality divine energy-intelligence can be molded and formed into any thought or idea that you choose. In the world of experience money seems to be changeable into any "thing" you may want or need. Money can provide you a chair, the best doctor, a trip to Europe, a lovely home, you name it! It seems like the money itself is the source of all your needs. It is easy to come to this conclusion. If you consider any outer channel to be your source of good, you establish limitation in your life. It is therefore necessary to consciously acknowledge God as your source. The conscious acknowledgement must be accompanied by an outer action, that of tithing. Your ability to tithe transcends the limiting appearance that any outer "thing" can be your source. With tithing comes the freedom to make choices according to what you know rather than according to what you can "afford". The act of tithing involves you in commitment to God. It places God first because you are seeking the prosperity consciousness over results. Of course, prosperous results follow, but it is the consciousness of well being and prosperity that you seek above all. The understanding and the act of tithing erases any belief that a salary, a boss, a condition, or a personality is your source of good.

To experience a genuine sense of well being you must feel it in your subconscious. This is where you hold your beliefs and store your memories. Prosperity and fear have their roots in your subconscious, so this is the area where you need to accept the truth of your being. That which you hold in your subconscious is what you produce in the outer, so you want to make sure that deep within, you feel prosperous and release any sense of limitation.

Denial and affirmation are wonderful tools for establishing and accepting the correct beliefs within your subconscious. Imagining is another way to initiate the living experience of feeling prosperous. Seeing yourself in a positive light with all your needs met helps you to bring it about. Setting goals and joyfully observing the step by step unfoldment taking place is another way to witness your inner change toward a prosperity consciousness. Act "as if" it were so and it will come to pass. The building of a prosperity consciousness requires a deliberate plan and an honest appraisel of how you feel about yourself. This helps you set a specific direction in learning the Truth about the Christ within. When you accept the wonderful truth that you are prosperity itself and that all your needs are met from within, you develop a sense of well being, a prosperity consciousness. At the same time you build your world into a living experience of plenty.

In order to develop spiritually and experience God, you must move God through you. To develop your awareness of love you must love by expressing it, by pressing it out. To develop your imagination you must exercise it. To develop strength you must demonstrate tolerance and steadfastness. The same holds true in developing a prosperity consciousness. To feel the inner flow of prosperity you must enter into the process of giving and receiving.

When you give, you automatically receive. This quickens your awareness of that which is moving through your consciousness. This is moving God through you and causing increase in your life. Of course, that which is given in love causes multiplied blessings in return and at the same time, erases fear of lack. You may wonder how much you need to give to properly develop a prosperity consciousness. Giving is a part of spiritual worship. Your gift must include with it a sense of release or surrender to God rather than outer things. It has been realized through the ages that increasing the gift to God causes an inner feeling of sacrifice until you reach the tithing level, that of ten percent. Then, there is the sense of fulfillment. The reason the tithe brings with it the prosperity consciousness is that it represents one hundred percent of your income. The tithe represents your willingness to give all. This goes far beyond the material; it holds true of all that you are. If you dedicate yourself completely to God, you need give only ten percent of your time, your money, your attention, etc. The number "one" represents a portion and "zero" represents endless. Therefore the number ten represents a never ending portion of yourself that you are willing to give. When you reach this tithing level you move into complete willingness to trust God as your absolute source of all your good. Even though you will experience many emotions and challenges in developing to this point, the results are the freedom from fear and lack.

Never save money! It is vital that the law of circulation, of giving and receiving, is not blocked by the choice to horde. Your money must be placed into the stream of activity or it will diminish and your sense of well being will fade. Perhaps you will need to accumulate a certain amount to invest a lump sum, but this still has the purpose of activity. The fear that you may run out of money so you must save for a rainy day will block the flow of your good. It is motivated by fear. You must not base your spiritual choices upon feelings of fear. Even a retirement plan should include with it a plan of activity rather than its being a nest egg that will be depleted. Never allow for limitation; keep it flowing.

There are three levels of giving. At one level you may give in order to have your needs met. Recognizing that your source is divine energy-intelligence and understanding the principles of tithing you may give in order that you may receive. Secondly, it is perfectly legitimate to increase your gift for increased return. This, too, is an absolute demonstration of faith. When this is coupled with affirmation, imagery, and praise, you get results. The third level of giving is for the pure joy of giving itself. This is likening yourself to God when you give for the experience itself. God is the giver of all and your giving cleanses and purifies your consciousness. Some people need to buy something new when they feel bad. But a sure way to find release from being locked inside yourself is to give of yourself. This places you back into the stream of God's activity and reveals the cause of your problem.

These three levels can be simultaneous experiences. The three motives of need, increase, and likeness are continuous experiences which enrich your life and develop your awareness of God as your one and only source of good.

Many people who were afraid that they couldn't afford to tithe found that they couldn't afford not to tithe. They eventually tithed themselves out of debt. Whether one is tithing on thirty dollars or three million dollars the challenge and the experience are just the same. The same inner decision is required, the same divine activity begins. Due to the fact that everyone is an individual, the details and conditions will be unique. But the underlying principles remain the same. God is your source and you must acknowledge this truth with all that you are in complete commitment and trust. As you do, you are free from any sense of lack or limitation. You are coming into the understanding, as a New Thought Christian, of how to become prosperous.

SCRIPTURES

"They shall prosper that love thee." (Ps. 122:6)

"Where your treasure is, there will your heart be also." (Mat. 6:21)

"Soul, thou hast much goods laid up for many years; take thine ease." (Lu. 12:19)

QUESTIONS

1. Is prosperity the accumulation of money?

2. Why does money seem to be an answer to problems?

3. What frees you from depending on the outer as your source?

4. How do you develop your understanding of prosperity?

5. What is meant by "move God through you"?

6. What does the tithe represent?

7. Should you save money?

8. What are the three levels of giving?

9. Are there times when you can't afford to tithe?

10. How are you developing your prosperity consciousness?

DENIAL   There is no lack in my life; Nothing can block my flow of good.

AFFIRMATION   Tremendous supply and large sums are flowing from God to and through me this instant.